Autumn

Signs of the Season
Around North America

Written by Mary Pat Finnegan   Illustrated by Jeremy Schultz

Content Advisor: Julie Dunlap, Ph.D. • Reading Advisor: Lauren A. Liang, M.A.
Literacy Education, University of Minnesota, Minneapolis, Minnesota

PICTURE WINDOW BOOKS
MINNEAPOLIS, MINNESOTA

For Scott, my friend and partner through the seasons—M.P.F.

The author would like to thank Meg Weesner, Chief of Science and Resources Management at Saguaro National Park, and Wilma Payne, teacher in the Iditarod Area School District, McGrath, Alaska.

Editor: Nadia Higgins
Designer: Melissa Voda
Page production: The Design Lab
The illustrations in this book were prepared digitally.

Picture Window Books
5115 Excelsior Boulevard
Suite 232
Minneapolis, MN 55416
1-877-845-8392
www.picturewindowbooks.com

Printed in the United States of America.

Library of Congress Cataloging-in-Publication Data
Finnegan, Mary Pat, 1961–
  Autumn : signs of the season around North America / written by Mary Pat Finnegan ; illustrated by Jeremy Schultz.
    p. cm. — (Through the seasons) Includes index.
  Summary: Examines how autumn brings observable changes in weather, nature, and people.
  ISBN 1-4048-0426-9 (pbk.)—ISBN 1-4048-0000-X (hardcover)
  1. Autumn—North America—Juvenile literature. [1. Autumn.] I. Schultz, Jeremy, ill. II. Title. III. Through the seasons (Minneapolis, Minn.)
  QB637.7 .F55 2003
  508.2—dc21   2002005840

One way to mark the seasons is by looking at the calendar. The calendar dates are based on Earth's yearly trip around the sun. In North America, autumn begins on September 22 or 23, when day and night are about the same length. Throughout autumn, the days keep getting shorter.

Another way to mark the seasons is to look around you at the changes in weather and nature. In North America, the first signs of autumn appear in the north, then move south. This book helps you see the signs of autumn in different places around North America.

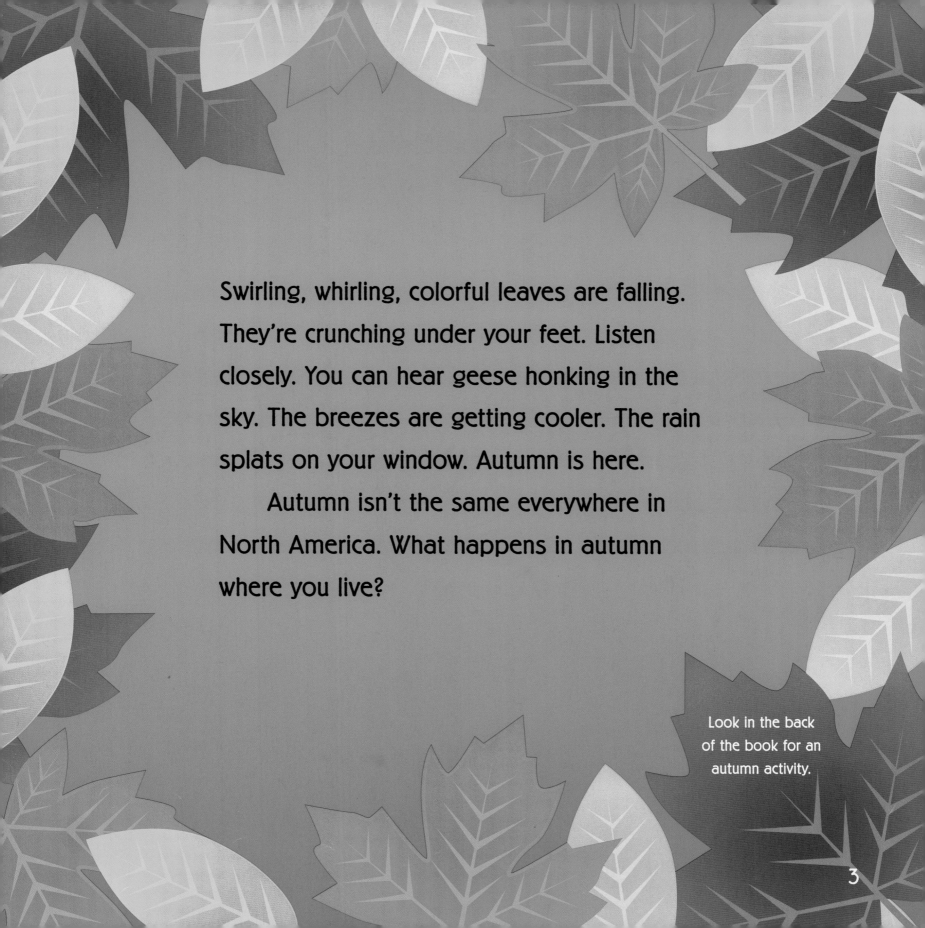

Swirling, whirling, colorful leaves are falling. They're crunching under your feet. Listen closely. You can hear geese honking in the sky. The breezes are getting cooler. The rain splats on your window. Autumn is here.

Autumn isn't the same everywhere in North America. What happens in autumn where you live?

Look in the back of the book for an autumn activity.

If you live in the far north, you'll see signs of autumn first. Each day, the sun rises later and later. Everything sparkles with frost.

4

In the evenings, the sun sets earlier and earlier.
The nights are colder. You know what's coming.
Soon there will be snow.

FUN FACT:
The farther north you live, the shorter the autumn
days. By the end of autumn in northern Canada and
Alaska, darkness has taken over nearly all of the day.

Grizzly bears feast on salmon and berries, then lumber off to their dens to hibernate. They will sleep until spring.

FUN FACT:
People in Alaska often see groups of caribou migrating.
The caribou are moving from their summer homes near
the Arctic Ocean to forests farther south.

See the flocks of birds in the sky. They are flying south.
Many birds migrate to warmer places in autumn.

In New England, you can feel the crisp autumn air soon after school starts. Breathe into the air on these cool days. You can see your breath!

Leaves are turning yellow, orange, red, and brown.

Everybody's raking the leaves into colorful piles.

Jump in!

FUN FACT:

Many leaves do not really make new colors. They lose color. As the days get shorter, the leaves stop making their green color, and orange and yellow then show through.

Munch, crunch, gnaw, peck. Mice and birds are fattening up. Little striped caterpillars eat and eat and eat. Soon they will change into beautiful monarch butterflies.

FUN FACT:
Monarch butterflies fly up to 3,000 miles (4,828 kilometers) to spend the winter in Mexico or California. That's a lot of flapping for a butterfly that weighs less than a penny!

Squirrels chase and chatter as they hide acorns and nuts.
They work hard now so they will have food in the winter.

Autumn is a busy time for farmers in the Midwest.

Giant combines move up and down the fields.

Harvest time is here.

Apples are crisp and juicy. Tables at the farmers' market are overflowing with potatoes, carrots, zucchini, tomatoes, and flowers.

FUN FACT:
The harvest moon is the full moon nearest to the first day of autumn. The moon is so big and bright that it helps farmers as they work into the night.

13

An autumn sunrise paints the sky purple and pink in the Appalachian Mountains. The dampness makes you shiver. Soon there will be rain.

Hunters are out with their dogs. You can hear the dogs howling as they run through the forest.

In California, you can spot humpback and blue whales as they make their way to winter homes.

Go for a boat ride. A young humpback whale might come right up to look at you. It's curious, too.

The desert air is hot and dry during the day. Seeds from desert broom plants drift together in the wind.

18

At night, it cools off. The desert wakes up. Rabbits, mice, and other animals are searching for food.

Now you know what autumn is like in different places around North America. What happens in autumn where you live?

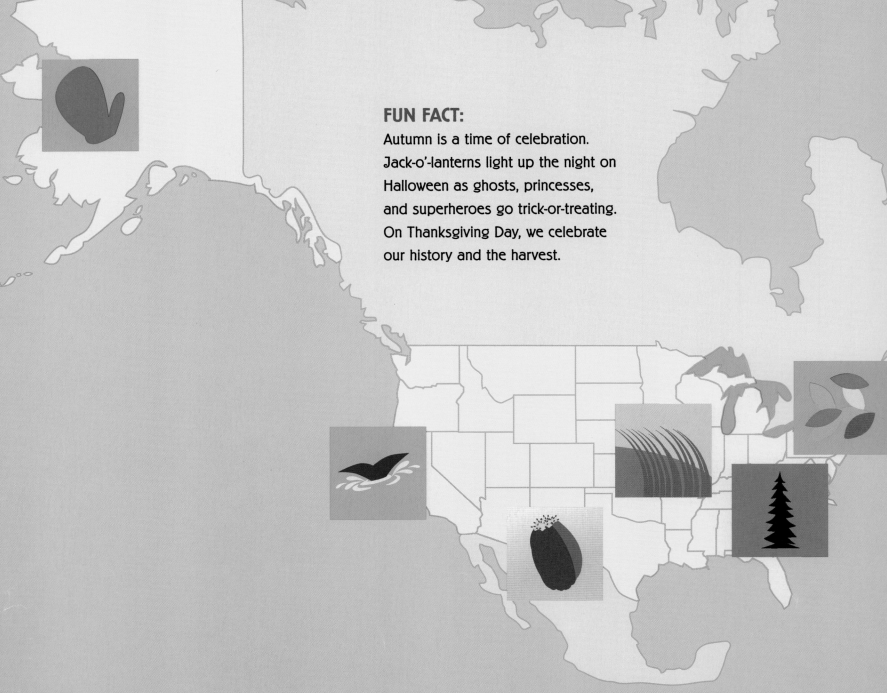

FUN FACT:

Autumn is a time of celebration. Jack-o'-lanterns light up the night on Halloween as ghosts, princesses, and superheroes go trick-or-treating. On Thanksgiving Day, we celebrate our history and the harvest.

ALASKA/NORTHERN CANADA

Fairbanks, Alaska
Average high November temperature: 11°F/-12°C
Hours of daylight on November 30th: 4 hours, 46 minutes
What to wear: parka, hat, mittens, boots
Signs of autumn: snowy days, smoke rising from chimneys

NEW ENGLAND

Portsmouth, New Hampshire
Average high November temperature: 48°F/9°C
Hours of daylight on November 30th: 9 hours, 16 minutes
What to wear: light winter coat
Sign of autumn: colorful leaves

MIDWEST

Dubuque, Iowa
Average high November temperature: 44°F/7°C
Hours of daylight on November 30th: 9 hours, 19 minutes
What to wear: light winter coat
Sign of autumn: harvest

APPALACHIAN MOUNTAINS

Asheville, North Carolina
Average high November temperature: 59°F/15°C
Hours of daylight on November 30th: 9 hours, 57 minutes
What to wear: jacket and sweater
Signs of autumn: dew, mist, and rain

CALIFORNIA COAST

Monterey, California
Average high November temperature: 66°F/19°C
Hours of daylight on November 30th: 9 hours, 51 minutes
What to wear: sweater or light jacket
Sign of autumn: blue and humpback whales

DESERTS

Nogales, Mexico
Average high November temperature: 71°F/22°C
Hours of daylight on November 30th: 10 hours, 17 minutes
What to wear: short sleeves
Sign of autumn: monarch butterflies flying overhead

Make a Pressed Leaf

You Will Need:

An adult to help you

Colorful, fresh leaves (Fallen leaves that have already started to dry
   will not work as well.)

An iron and ironing board

2 pieces of wax paper, each about 18 inches (about $\frac{1}{2}$ meter) long

2 towels

Lay a towel on the ironing board and smooth it flat. (This will keep any wax from getting on the ironing board.) Lay one piece of wax paper (waxy side up) on the towel. Arrange several leaves on the wax paper, making sure to leave space between the leaves. Lay the other piece of wax paper down (waxy side down) on top of the leaves. Think of it as a leaf sandwich. Lay the other towel over the wax paper. Have an adult press it with a warm iron. Your pressed leaf will keep its bright color for a long time.

Words to Know

autumn—the season between summer and winter. In North America, autumn lasts from the end of September to the end of December.

harvest moon—the full moon nearest the first day of autumn

hibernate—to spend the winter in a deep sleep

migrate—to travel regularly from one place to another in autumn and spring

To Learn More

AT THE LIBRARY

Hall, Zoe. *Fall Leaves Fall!* New York: Scholastic Press, 2000.

Robbins, Ken. *Autumn Leaves.* New York: Scholastic Press, 1998.

Rylant, Cynthia. *In November.* San Diego: Harcourt Brace, 2000.

Saunders-Smith, Gail. *Autumn.* Mankato, Minn.: Pebble Books, 1998.

Stille, Darlene R. *Fall.* Minneapolis: Compass Point Books, 2001.

ON THE WEB

U.S. Naval Observatory

http://www.usno.navy.mil

For sunrise and sunset times in cities around the world

National Oceanic and Atmospheric Administration Education Resources

http://www.education.noaa.gov

Activities, safety tips, and articles on weather for teachers and students

Want to learn more about autumn? Visit FACT HOUND at *http://www.facthound.com.*

Index